MONEY MATTERS

Loans and Credit

A Teen Guide to Borrowing

JENNIFER SANDERSON

Published in 2026 by **Cheriton Children's Books**
1 Bank Drive West, Shrewsbury, Shropshire, SY3 9DJ, UK

First Edition

Author: Jennifer Sanderson
Designer: Paul Myerscough
Editor: Kelly Short
Proofreader: Amy Strauss

Picture credits: Cover: Molibdenis Studio. Illustrations throughout by Molibdenis Studio. Inside: p4: Shutterstock/Mishchenko Svitlana, p5: Shutterstock/Fizkes, p6: Shutterstock/VH Studio, p7: Shutterstock/Syedfahadghazanfar, p8: Shutterstock/Dmitry Molchanov, p9: Shutterstock/Max Kegfire, p10: Shutterstock/Fizkes, p11: Shutterstock/New Africa, p12: Shutterstock/Pikselstock, p13: Shutterstock/M Agency, p14: Shutterstock/GaudiLab, p15: Shutterstock/Sichon, p16: Shutterstock/Jose Calsina, p18: Shutterstock/N Universe, p19: Shutterstock/TierneyMJ, pp20-21: Shutterstock/Gorodenkoff, p22: Shutterstock/Zamrznuti Tonovi, p23: Shutterstock/Pui Bunny, p24: Shutterstock/ProstockStudio, p25: Shutterstock/Maxbelchenko, p26: Shutterstock/PeopleImages.com/Yuri A, p27: Shutterstock/Just Life, p29: Shutterstock/Rafa Jodar, p31: Shutterstock/Prostock Studio, pp32-33: Shutterstock/Krakenimages.com, p34: Shutterstock/Lopolo, p36: Shutterstock/Mavo, p37: Shutterstock/Ground Picture, p38: Shutterstock/PeopleImages.com/Yuri A, p39: Shutterstock/Dean Drobot, p40: Shutterstock/Fizkes, p42: Shutterstock/Paul Brennan, p43: Shutterstock/Chay Tee, pp44-45: Shutterstock/Fast Stock.

Printed in China

Please visit our website,
www.cheritonchildrensbooks.com
to see more of our high-quality books.

Contents

CHAPTER 1

Why Money Matters

Have you ever heard the saying, "Money makes the world go round?" It means that money is the most important thing in the world. While money may not be *the* most important thing in the world, the truth is money really does matter to everyone. Almost everything we do is affected by how much money we have and need to have.

Simple Spends

The things you spend money on now are simple, but as you grow older money matters become more complicated. And as an adult, the things you need become bigger and more expensive. For example, you'll likely spend money on cars, property, and things you need every day, such as food. Once those things are paid for, you can buy the things you'd like. But whatever your age, the skills you need to manage your money are the same. Working on those skills now is a great way to make sure you are ready to handle your finances in the future.

When you want new clothes, shoes, or gadgets, how much you buy and where you buy it from depends on how much money you have.

Money matters can be confusing. If you need help, ask questions. The more you know, the better!

Money Need to Know

Many teens say that they worry about money. In fact, around 54 percent say that thinking about finances makes them anxious. They say they do not feel that they are taught enough about money at school. About 42 percent of teens say they have had no money-management classes in school, and 73 percent say they would take courses in money management if available. There is a big gap in financial education for teens. This book will set out to help deal with that lack of education. It will give you the tools you need to feel confident about handling money and building your financial future.

Money Skills

With some simple financial skills, it is easy to get a grip on your money. You can also develop those skills further. Some key financial skills include:

- Budgeting
- Saving
- Investing
- Earning
- Managing debt
- Managing credit
- Setting financial goals
- Understanding tax
- Learning about insurance
- Getting to grips with risk and return

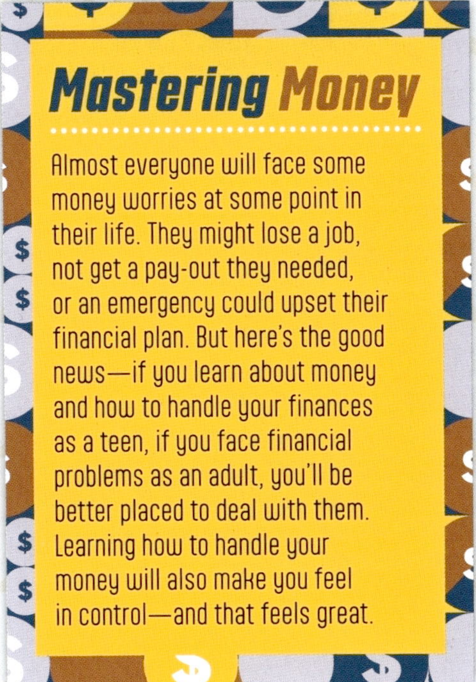

Mastering Money

Almost everyone will face some money worries at some point in their life. They might lose a job, not get a pay-out they needed, or an emergency could upset their financial plan. But here's the good news—if you learn about money and how to handle your finances as a teen, if you face financial problems as an adult, you'll be better placed to deal with them. Learning how to handle your money will also make you feel in control—and that feels great.

Being financially literate helps you make important financial decisions.

Learning about Financial Literacy

If you are someone who hasn't spent a lot of time thinking about finances so far, this book is as much for you as it is for someone who is very financially literate. Being financially literate means understanding basic things to do with money. That includes budgeting, saving, debt, credit, and investing. It covers managing risk, planning for the future, and knowing about tax. It also means being able to recognize when something is too financially good to be true! Everyone needs to be financially literate these days to navigate modern life and get the most from their money.

Making It Work for You

When you are financially literate, you can have a healthy and smart relationship with money. You understand how to make money work for you. With financial literacy you will not be confused when people use the language of money. By the end of this book, we will have covered many key financial terms, and explained them, so you'll be well placed to handle any conversations about money in the future. Financial literacy gives you the tools you need to understand important information such as the details about a loan.

The Key to Freedom

One of the greatest gifts that financial literacy will give you is a sense of control and freedom. When you are financially literate you understand the world of money. That helps you make good decisions and good choices about how to spend your money. You can choose where to save your money. If you do decide to borrow money at any point, perhaps by using a credit card or getting a loan, you will be able to understand the deals on offer and choose the best one. You will also understand the language attached to lending, so you know exactly what you are getting yourself into.

You don't need to be great at math to master simple money skills, and money doesn't have to be complicated. In this book, we'll try to make it as simple and easy to understand as possible. We'll take the mystery out of money and the fear away from finances. We'll show you how money can be exciting and give you freedom, and how it can help you shape your future.

Teens and Money

In today's digital world, most stores are online. And tech-savvy teens buy many of the things they want and need online. While this is convenient, it also makes it easy to overspend. Many teens say they are tempted to buy online because of advertising. It's also an incredibly easy way to shop. With just a few clicks and taps, you can spend a lot very quickly. But that's a quick way to get into debt.

It's very easy to overspend, so keep track of your online shopping.

How to Use Credit

In this book we will explore the financial skill of using credit in a smart way. We'll also look at how to avoid unmanageable debt. These skills are important now but they will become even more crucial when you are older. If you learn now how credit works and how to use it effectively, as an adult you will be financially smarter.

Debt Free, Stress Free

Being in debt is not just about the money. It can also have a bad effect on your mental health. Constantly worrying about money can leave you feeling anxious, stressed, and overwhelmed. If you feel stressed for a long period of time, this can lead to depression.

Taking an amazing vacation that you can't really afford and that leaves you in unmanageable debt is not fun in the long run.

Mastering Money

Sometimes, it's much easier to borrow money from friends or family than to try to apply for a bank loan. Around 20 percent of US adults get financial help from friends and family. But borrowing money from friends and family can put a strain on the relationship. It can cause arguments because the person who lent the money would like the money repaid but the borrower can't pay it back or doesn't want to. This can lead to an upsetting breakdown in the relationship.

Anyone who borrows money from friends and family needs to set up a proper agreement with the lender. They also need a repayment plan to figure out how and when the loan will be paid back. In the same way, lenders need to think carefully before agreeing to any loans, and should set a schedule for repayments too.

Steps to Financial Freedom

We'll explore how to be credit-wise now, while you are a teenager, and we'll also take a look at your future and the type of money management you'll need to work on as an adult. Along the way, we'll cover advice from financial experts, so that you can learn to manage your money like a pro. So, are you ready to make money work for you? Then let's get started.

Being smart with your money feels great. The more you learn now as a teen, the easier managing your finances will be as an adult.

CHAPTER 2

The Basics of Credit

Buying your first car or home is a big deal. A basic new car costs around $20,000. According to realtors, today the average house costs nearly $450,000, depending on the state. Whichever way you look at it, that's a lot of money. So how do people afford such expensive things? The answer is simple: by using credit.

Borrowers and Lenders

Credit is an agreement between a borrower and a lender. It works like this: The borrower gets money or something of value, and commits to repaying the lender later. Credit and debt work together. Your credit is the total amount of money you can borrow. It's also called your limit. Debt is the amount of money you owe. If you have a credit card with a limit of $1,000 and you spend $400 on it, you are $400 in debt. When you pay back the money, you are no longer in debt. Your debt is usually lower than your credit.

Buying a property puts most people in debt. But if you budget and buy a home that you can afford, you will be able to manage the repayments.

A good credit utilization ratio is below 30 percent.

Figuring It Out

To figure out if a person is on track and using their credit wisely, lenders calculate the person's credit utilization ratio. This is sometimes called a debt-to-limit ratio. It is the amount of debt the person owes as a percentage of the credit they have. For example, if a person has two credit cards with $5,000 limits, their limit is $5,000 x 2, so $10,000 in total. If they owe $2,500 on each card ($2,500+$2,500), that makes a total debt of $5,000 out of a possible $10,000. You calculate their credit utilization ratio by saying: $5,000 ÷ $10,000 = 0.5. To get this as a percentage, you'd say 0.5 x 100 = 50. Their credit utilization ratio is 50 percent.

Mastering Money

Anyone over the age of 18 can apply for credit. They will be asked questions and will usually need to provide certain documents. These include pay stubs and W-2 forms (these are forms you are sent at the end of each tax year to show what you've earned). They also include recent bank statements. Applicants also need to supply their Social Security Number. Once the lender has all the information, they review the case. They also look at the person's credit history and rating—we'll look at these in detail later. Before they say yes or no to an application, lenders must comply with the Equal Credit Opportunity Act (ECOA). To comply means they follow the rules. This law makes sure they don't discriminate against applicants based on their race, religion, sex, whether they're married, and other factors.

Different Types of Credit

Next up we'll look at the types of credit you can get. It's important to understand them because they affect how you pay back a loan. There are two different types of credit: revolving and installment. They differ, depending on how the money is paid back to the lender.

Revolving Credit

In revolving credit, you borrow money, pay it back, and borrow again. You can borrow as little or as much as you like, within your limit. There's no fixed end date for when your credit ends, so revolving credit is also sometimes called open-ended credit. It's also called unsecured debt. This is because there is no collateral needed. Collateral is something you give as security for the repayment. Collateral might be a home, for example. Revolving credit examples include credit card accounts and lines of credit. A line of credit is a set amount of money that borrowers are given. They can use as much or as little of the line of credit as they need. In a Home Equity Line of Credit (HELOC) people borrow large sums of money and use their home as collateral.

Last year, on average each borrower owed $6,380 on their credit card. Gen Z (18 to 25 years old) owed the least money, while Gen X (42 to 57 years old) owed the most. On average this was more than $8,000.

Just about every household has some type of debt. At the end of 2025, US households owed on average $105,056. Around 70 percent of this debt is from home loans.

Installment Credit

In installment credit, the borrower receives a one-off lump sum of money. Often this lump sum is very big. For example, it might be enough to buy a home or car. For that reason, the money has to be paid back in installments. The installments are equal amounts of money paid back over a set period of time. When the loan is paid off, the borrower is no longer in debt.

Paying Back the Loans

Whatever the type of credit you have, you will need to pay it back to keep your debt to a minimum. You may not realize it, but lenders don't just hand out money, it always comes at a price. That price is the interest added to the repayments or total debt.

Teens and Money

Many teens say they worry about building up debt they can't repay, especially with credit cards or loans. They also say they worry about how debt might affect their future, for example, with buying a home. Learning to manage credit and debt as a teenager can take away those fears.

Before you take out any type of credit, it's important to figure out the interest you'll have to pay. Interest can add up to a lot over time.

What Is Interest?

When you borrow money, the amount of money you borrow is called the principal. When you pay it back, you pay back the principal, plus interest. The interest is calculated as a percentage of the amount borrowed. There are two different types of interest: simple and compound.

Understanding Simple Interest

Simple interest is when a lender charges a fixed yearly fee for borrowing money. The total interest depends on the length of time it takes for the loan to be repaid. You can calculate the simple interest like this:

Simple interest = P x R x N

- P = principal amount
- R = annual interest rate, written as a decimal
- N = term of loan in years

Let's look at an example. If you borrow $100, the interest rate is 10 percent, and you agree to pay back the loan after 5 years, your calculation looks like this:

- Simple interest = 100 x 0.10 x 5
- The simple interest will be $50

The total amount that you will repay is: $100 + $50 = $150.

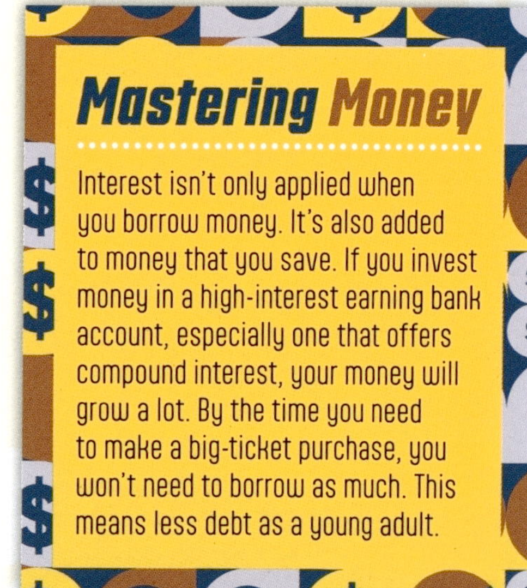

Mastering Money

Interest isn't only applied when you borrow money. It's also added to money that you save. If you invest money in a high-interest earning bank account, especially one that offers compound interest, your money will grow a lot. By the time you need to make a big-ticket purchase, you won't need to borrow as much. This means less debt as a young adult.

Understanding Compound Interest

Compound interest is a lot more complicated because it accrues, or builds, over time. You pay interest on the principal and the interest that has accumulated, or built up. Interest can be compounded daily, monthly, quarterly, or annually. The more often it's compounded, the more you'll pay. The formula for compound interest is:

Compound interest = $P \times (1+r)^t - P$

- P = principal amount
- r = annual interest rate, written as a decimal
- t= number of years interest is applied

So, if you borrow $100 at an interest rate of 10 percent over 5 years, this is the calculation:

- Compound interest = $100 \times (1+0.10)^5 - 100$

$= 100 \times (1.10)^5 - 100$

$= 100 \times 1.6105 - 100$

$= 161.05 - 100$

$= 61.05$

In this case, the total you'd pay is $100 + 61.05 = $161.05. As you can see from the examples above, simple interest costs a lot less than compound interest.

If you're still putting your savings in a piggy bank, it's time to open a bank account that will earn you high interest.

Get Financially Fit:

Building Credit like a Pro

Expert Tips!

Building good credit is important. Good credit means having a strong track record of managing money responsibly, and particularly when borrowing and repaying. It tells lenders that you're financially sound. The better your credit, the better your chances of loans for big purchases like homes and cars. Good credit will also give you a better interest rate when you apply for a loan. So how do you build good credit? Here are some insider tips from financial experts.

Using your credit card wisely can help you manage your finances.

Always Pay Up

You may not have a lot of bills as a teenager but once you do, you need to pay them on time. Credit facilities look for at least six months of bills paid on time. If you're a bit forgetful, set up an auto-pay on your banking app so that money automatically comes off your account. You could also set up calendar reminders so you remember to pay your bills and keep on track.

Always Pay Off

If you have revolving credit, like a credit card, pay off as much as you can each time. Ideally, if you budget properly, you should be able to pay off the whole balance each month.

Keep Them Open

Don't close bank accounts. The longer you've had bank accounts for, the better. This is especially true for credit card accounts. If you have a credit card that you don't use, keep it active by buying something small. But remember to pay it off as soon as you can.

Mix It Up

It's a good idea to have a mix of credit, for example, a credit card and a credit-builder loan. A credit-builder loan is a specific type of loan designed to help people build credit. It often comes with a high-interest rate but sometimes, if payments are met on time and the loan is paid in full, the interest may be refunded, or paid back to the borrower.

Only Apply When You Really Need It

Lenders can see each time you apply for credit, so don't apply unless you need to. They'll notice if you apply for a lot of credit in a short space of time. That tells them that you have unmanageable debt.

What Are Credit Scores?

The main reason to build your credit is to make sure you get a good credit score or rating on your credit report. A credit report is just like a school report: It tracks your progress. Credit reports are used by banks and other lenders, insurance companies, landlords, and some employers. They use them to see how creditworthy you are. That means how likely you are to repay your debts, which shows what your risk to lenders would be.

Getting a Good Score

The Fair Isaac Corp (FICO) created the credit-score system. Today there are other scoring systems but FICO is used by 90 percent of lenders. Just like your school report is made up of different test grades, there are several factors that influence your score. One of the most important is your payment history and if you've paid your bills on time. If you've made late payments, the later they were, the worse your score will be. They also look at your credit utilization ratio —go back to page 11 if you need a recap on how this works. A higher ratio means you earn fewer points. If you've had credit for a long time, that's a good thing. And if you have a mix of credit, it shows that you can manage your debt. How many times you've applied for credit also has a negative affect on your score.

The FICO Score

Once all these factors have been taken into account, you get a FICO score. These range from 300 to 850:

- 800 to 850 is exceptional
- 740 to 799 is very good
- 670 to 739 is good
- 580 to 669 is fair
- Lower than 579 is poor

If you have a high score, you are more likely to be offered more credit. You may get a better interest rate, which will save you money in the long run. If you have a low score, it can be a problem, but it's fixable. You can try to build good credit—go back to the previous pages for some tips. Building credit can take around six months. If you don't have time, you could work with a credit repair company. They will offer you advice and talk to credit agencies on your behalf too.

Mastering Money

There are three main credit bureaus: TransUnion, Experian, and Equifax. You are entitled to one free credit report at each of them, each year. All you need to do is log on at annualcreditreport.com.

It's important to check your credit report carefully to make sure there are no errors. If there are, you need to report them immediately.

Check your credit report at least once a year. If you see that your score is low, you can take steps to improve it.

Credit and Debt Made Easy

There was a lot of financial information in this chapter, and a large amount of that will be new to you. There were probably many words and terms you didn't know, so let's recap what you've learned.

Borrowers, Lenders, and Credit

Credit is an agreement between a borrower and a lender. The lender (usually a bank or credit union) loans the borrower money. The borrower promises to pay back that money within a certain time frame.

Owing Money

The money that you owe, is your debt. The amount of debt you have in relation to how much credit you have is called your credit-utilization ratio. The lower this is, the better.

Types of Credit

In revolving credit, you have an amount of credit you can use as and when you need it. In installment credit, you promise to pay off a principal amount over a set period.

Interest Matters

For credit facilities to make a profit from lending you money, they charge interest. Interest can be simple or compound. Simple interest works out lower than compound interest, so it's better when borrowing money. Compound interest is better for saving.

Building Good Credit

You need to build good credit to have a high credit score. The higher your score, the better. Credit scores affect your ability to get more credit. They can affect your ability to rent a property. Some employers also check your credit score.

CHAPTER 3

How to Manage Credit

The simplest way to build your credit is with revolving credit. This includes credit card accounts, retail or store credit cards, secured credit cards, and student credit cards. But how do these different cards work? Keep reading!

What Are Credit Cards?

Today, most adults have credit cards. You can be an authorized user on someone else's credit card account from as young as 13. This means you have a card in your name, but it's not your account. The person who holds the account is responsible for the payments. When you turn 18, you're legally allowed your own account. That's exciting! But it does mean that you'll be responsible for the payments. You'll need to understand how credit cards work so that you don't find yourself in a lot of debt.

Credit cards can be useful for buying things you want, but only if you manage them well.

How Credit Cards Work

When you use a credit card to pay for something, you don't get charged immediately. Instead, the bank pays for your purchase, and at the end of each month, the bank sends you a statement, or list of what you've spent. The statement also gives you a minimum amount to pay. If you only pay the minimum, you will be charged interest on the rest of the debt. If you don't pay anything, you will be charged penalties too. Penalties are a little like punishments and they can worsen your credit score.

Shopping Around

To open a credit card account, you'll need to provide proof of identity, age, and income. Most banks will want you to have a specific credit score or higher. The interest rates that banks offer on their accounts are different from bank to bank, so you'll need to shop around for the best deal. You want the account that offers you the lowest interest rate and the most perks. Perks may include loyalty points for each purchase, which you can swap for cash.

Teens and Money

From gaming consoles to clothes, teens buy a lot of things. Credit card companies are smart and they've realized this. They've designed cards especially for young adults. They lure young adults with great deals on credit cards. They also target teens by playing on their parents' emotions. The companies say that having a credit card is a good way to learn about credit and to grow credit. This is true, and parents want their children to understand finances. So parents often give their teens a card attached to theirs. But, if young adults and teens are not taught how to manage their credit, these cards can turn into a debt trap.

Just as you shop around for goods, so you need to shop around for the best rates on a credit card account.

It's reported that 26 million US adults don't have credit history. This makes having regular credit cards difficult. For these adults, using retail cards to build credit may be a good idea.

What Are Retail Cards?

Another way to build credit is to get a retail card. There are two types of retail card: store credit cards and co-branded credit cards. Store credit cards are credit cards that allow you to buy things at one particular store or chain of stores. They are called closed-loop cards. Co-branded credit cards are credit cards that you can use anywhere, not just in one particular chain of stores. They are linked to either the Visa or Mastercard network. They can be used wherever you see those signs. Some retailers, such as Amazon, offer store credit cards and co-branded credit cards. Each has its own individual perks.

Big Benefits

The benefits of having a retail card are usually not as good as a standard credit card. For example, the interest rate is usually much higher. But retail cards are easier to get compared to regular credit cards. They're a good way to build credit quickly too. When you shop at the store associated with the card, you will also likely get discounts and special offers. For example, if you have a Target card, you get 5 percent off all your purchases. This is an easy way to save yourself some money and build credit at the same time. That's a win-win for you!

Mastering Money

Some people sign up for retail cards for the perks, from regular discounts to in-store coupons. But if your goal is to save money when you shop, there may be a better way to do this: You could sign up for a shopping app instead. Stores pay shopping apps for bringing customers their way, so the apps pass on part of the payment to customers. Rakuten and RetailMeNot are good examples of this. You sign up for the service and shop using promo codes, coupons, and cashback deals.

Not All Good

Having a wallet full of retail cards may look impressive, but it really isn't! You don't need a retail card for every store you usually shop at. The main reason for avoiding this is because too many cards can lower your credit score. It's also incredibly easy to spend a little on each card—and before you know it, you'll be in a lot of debt. Store cards typically charge high interest rates so it's a great idea to pay off your balance in full each month to avoid interest charges. If you can't do this, make sure you budget properly.

If you regularly shop at the same store, a retail card is a good way to save a little each time you shop.

Secured Credit Cards

If retail cards are not for you and you're not eligible for a regular credit card, you could consider a secured credit card. These are similar to regular credit cards but instead of the bank giving you a limit, you make a cash deposit. That deposit becomes the limit for your account. You use the card like a regular credit card.

Secured credit cards don't give you the best interest rate and there may also be hidden charges. However, they're a good way to slowly build credit. Once your credit score has improved, you could apply for a regular credit card. When you close your account, you'll get back your deposit. If you're smart, you'll save this money for a rainy day. (That means, when you really need it!)

Credit Cards for Students

Student credit cards are specifically for students and work just like regular credit cards. Banks realize that students likely don't necessarily have high credit scores, or even one at all, so you don't need any credit history to successfully apply. You also don't need to be a full-time student. These credit cards are unsecured. This means that you don't need collateral or a security deposit either to get the card.

Coming with Rewards

The biggest advantage of a student credit card is that you can build credit before you start full-time work. You'll also be able to use your card for emergencies—from unplanned flights to see a sick family member or a car repair you didn't budget for. Some cards give you a percentage of cashback on your purchases too. This can be as much as 5 percent.

Some issuers cancel your student credit card after graduation.

Spend wisely on your credit card to ensure your credit utilization ration stays as low as possible.

Don't Ignore the Risks!

Do student credit cards sound too good to be true? Perhaps they are! Student credit cards come with high interest charges. If you don't manage your account carefully, it's very easy to spiral into debt. After you graduate, some credit card issuers will transfer your account to a standard card. This means you'll likely get more credit but it also means that you could go further into debt if you don't budget well.

Teens and Money

According to research, around 60 percent of students have credit cards. The average student credit card debt is around $3,000. That may not seem like a lot but the average credit card limit is $3,500. This means their credit utilization ratio is 85 percent. When it comes to their credit score, a ratio of more than 30 percent can affect the rating.

Get Financially Fit:

Manage Your Credit Card like a Pro

Expert Tips!

It can be really exciting when you get your first credit card. It's a big step toward financial independence and freedom. But, with freedom comes responsibility. Any credit account, no matter the type, needs to be carefully managed to prevent you going into unmanageable debt. Here's what the experts say about managing revolving credit.

Keep Track

It's really easy to overspend on a credit card—after all, you're really just tapping and going. To save yourself from getting a nasty surprise when your statement arrives, keep track of what you're spending. With banking apps, this is easy to do. Some apps even let you set up notifications to warn you when you're nearing your limit.

Pay It All

To make sure you stay ahead of the interest game, set up a reminder so that you pay your entire bill each month. You can also set up an auto-payment to pay something each month. This will mean you'll never have to pay penalty charges for missing a payment.

Having a credit card makes it very tempting to buy whatever you want, but you still need to budget for it.

Big Purchases and Emergencies

When it comes to buying large items, calculate how much you have to spend and make a timeline to pay off the bill. Always ask yourself, "Is the interest worth it?" If you go ahead, be sharp about paying off your bill. Add the amount to your budget (there's more about this on the next page) and set up an auto-payment with the amount you want to pay. Try to pay off the full amount as soon as possible.

Say No to More Credit

If you're managing your credit card account well, it's possible that your bank may ask you if you want to up your limit. Think hard, do you really need the higher limit? In many cases, it isn't necessary and it may just encourage you to overspend.

Do You Really Need the Perks?

As you earn more money, you'll likely be offered a new-and-improved credit card, one with more benefits. These may include things like travel insurance and being able to use airport lounges—but remember, nothing is free! You'll likely pay higher fees to have the improved card, so always ask yourself, "Do I really need the extra perks?" If you don't, pass.

Watch Out for Scammers!

There are so many different types of scam and unfortunately, many are linked to banking. Keep your credit card safe and never give your details to anyone. Know what you're spending so that you can check your statement. You can also set up notifications on your banking app each time your card is used. If you see that something's not right, contact your bank immediately.

Setting a Budget

When you have a credit card, it doesn't mean you can spend whatever you like. You need to plan so that you don't get into unmanageable debt. The best way to do this is by setting a budget.

Know Your Income

The first step is to know what's coming into your bank account. That's your income. If you get an allowance, it's income. If you earn a wage or salary, that's income too. Add together all your income.

Know Your Expenses

Your expenses are what you spend money on. Figuring out all your expenses can be complicated. An easy way to do this is to go through your bank statements and group all the same types of spending together—for example, clothes purchases, outings, and subscriptions. Add up what each type comes to. Then write down your total.

Save Some Money

As part of your budget, set aside some money as savings. This means that if you have an emergency, you won't need to max your credit card. If you invest wisely now, that money could grow by the time you need it.

Do the Math

Subtract your expenses and your savings from your total income. If you end up with a difference of 0, that's great! If you have money left over, that's even better. Instead of spending the extra money, consider upping your savings.

Some experts say you should allocate 60 percent of your income to needs, 20 percent to wants, and 20 percent to savings.

If you have expenses that are higher than your income, it's time to cut costs. Could you spend less on clothing or stay in a little more? Rather than always buying things on your credit card, save a little each month toward those items. Saving and buying things later will give you a sense of satisfaction—and stop you getting into debt.

Mastering Money

If you find that you're spending too much money, here are some smart and simple ways to cut back:

- **Think carefully about big purchases:** Can you go without that item until you've saved for some or all of it? Will it add value to your life that outweighs its financial burden?
- **Plan for things:** Don't spend on the fly, rather, plan carefully and stay within your budget.
- **Aim for a lower credit utilization ratio:** Set yourself a lower limit and try to stick to it. This will make it easier to pay off the bill in full each month.
- **Try a spending freeze**: Don't spend money on anything that's unnecessary.
- **Shop around:** Don't just buy the first item because it's easy. Do some research and see if you can get it cheaper elsewhere.

Another way to cut back on expenses is to limit your subscriptions: You really don't need two music subscriptions and six streaming subscriptions! Pick one of each instead.

Credit Cards Made Easy

In this chapter we looked at types of revolving credit and how to manage them. Some of the information will not be relevant right now but it's important to understand it to give you greater financial confidence when you're older. Here is a recap.

Credit Cards Have Pros and Cons

A credit card is useful for paying for big-ticket items and unexpected emergencies. But always remember that credit cards come with high interest rates. It's best to pay off as much of your bill as possible to avoid interest. If you forget to pay your bill, you'll get hit with penalties and lose points on your credit score.

Retail Cards Come with Perks

Store credit cards can only be used in the specific store or chain of stores. Co-branded retail cards can be used elsewhere too. With both types of card, you'll get good discounts but it's also easy to overspend and get into debt.

Spend with a Secured Credit Card

Secured credit cards don't always offer decent interest rates but they are good for building credit when you have no credit history. You pay a security deposit, which acts as your credit limit, and then use your card like a regular credit card.

Credit Cards Just for Students

Student credit cards are tailor-made for young adults who are at college. They offer all the benefits of a regular credit card but are easier to get. They often come with good perks that can boost your finances.

Pay Your Bills

Because credit cards come with high interest rates, you need to pay as much of your bill as possible to avoid paying interest. Tips to do this include keeping track of your spends, keeping your credit utilization ratio low, and staying safe to avoid being scammed.

Budget Smart to Avoid Debt

It's very easy to overspend on a credit card and land up in debt. To stay financially fit, you need to set up a budget. This means monitoring your income and expenses. As part of your expenses, you should also set aside some money and save it. This will help avoid going into debt when there's an emergency that requires money or a big spend.

CHAPTER 4

How to Use Credit in the Future

Revolving credit may be the first credit most people use, but at some stage, you'll need installment credit. Installment credit is for life's REALLY BIG purchases, such as cars, homes, and education.

What Is Installment Credit?

We mentioned installment credit earlier, but let's do a quick recap. With installment credit, the borrower receives a lump sum of money that must be paid back over time. The money is paid back in regular installments. The money you borrow is called the principal. The length of time you have to pay it back is called the term. The term can vary from weeks to decades. Installment credit includes home loans, auto loans, and personal loans. It also includes student loans and mortgages on property.

Installment credit is often linked to secured debt, which is also known as collateralized debt. This means that the borrower has something of value to back up the debt. For example, with an auto loan, you'd promise the vehicle as collateral. If you don't pay the loan, the lender can seize the car.

It's great to have your own car but you have to keep up with the loan repayments.

How an Installment Loan Works

When you apply for an installment loan, the lender will check to see that you meet their minimum requirements. You'll need proof of ID, pay stubs, bank statements, and proof of address. Lenders will also check your credit score to figure out how creditworthy you are. Installment credit lenders often want higher credit scores than revolving credit lenders. This is because the amount of money borrowed is usually much more.

If you're successful, you'll need to sign a loan agreement. The agreement will cover the principal, the term, the interest rate, and any fees. The interest rate will depend on how much you're borrowing and your credit score. It may be a fixed interest rate or one that changes. A changing interest rate is known as variable. Each month, your repayment will include a portion of the capital plus the interest that's built up since your last payment. You'll keep paying that amount until you have paid back the entire loan.

Mastering Money

In some installment loans, you can choose the term of your loan. Some people will opt for a longer term to give them lower repayments. This means they'll more easily pay the installments. Other people will pay off a higher amount over a shorter period of time. This means over time, they'll pay a lot less in interest. Whatever option borrowers choose, they have to pay the installments each month. Failure to do so, will see penalties or even the collateral seized. This will also have a negative effect on their credit score.

Budgeting and Installment Credit

Installment credit makes budgeting straightforward. This is because the installment won't change from month to month if the interest rate is fixed. You pay the same amount, month after month, until the loan is paid off and you're debt free. It's much easier to plan for this expense.

Installment credit also has much lower interest rates than revolving credit. For example, on a credit card, the average interest rate is more than 20 percent but an installment loan on a home sees borrowers paying only around 6.5 percent interest.

Taking Out a Personal Loan

A personal loan is installment credit. It can be used for many things, from paying for a wedding and upgrading your home to paying medical bills. Personal loans are usually unsecured, so they don't require collateral. But that means that the interest rates can be much higher. Some are more than 35 percent, depending on the borrower's credit score. The terms of personal loans vary from one to seven years. But, before you take out a personal loan, think carefully. If you're taking out a loan for a luxury, do you really need that item? And is it worth the debt?

It's a good idea to meet with an advisor to make sure you have budgeted properly for your big purchases.

Buying a Car

For many people, a car is essential. But cars are also very expensive and few people can afford to pay cash for their car. Instead, they use an auto loan to buy it. Auto loans use the vehicle as collateral to secure the debt—if people don't pay the installments, the lender can repossess the vehicle. Many auto loans require a down payment. That's a lump sum that the borrower pays up front. The down payment reduces the monthly installments. Always be sure to read the fine print of any loan: Some auto loans have a prepayment penalty. This is a charge if you pay off the vehicle before you're meant to. Lenders have these penalties in place to make sure that they don't lose out on interest payments.

Teens and Money

More than 100 million people have auto loans in the United States. The total auto debt in 2025 was over $1.66 trillion. Auto loans for teens are tough to come by, mostly because minors (people under the age of 18) cannot enter into legal contracts. Most often, an adult will need to cosign the contract. This makes the adult legally responsible for the loan repayments, so some adults may be repaying two cars at a time!

Taking a student loan is necessary for most students. Experts believe that it's better to take a loan and study than not go to college because you can't afford it.

Loans for Education

Education can be very expensive. After mortgages, student loans are the most common loans taken out. Student loans are specially designed to help students pay for education. There are different types of student loans—including federal and private.

Federal Student Loans

The US government helps students finance their higher education by offering federal student loans. These loans offer fixed interest rates, which are generally lower than private loans. Repayments usually begin only once the borrower starts working full time. The repayment amounts are often flexible with different options depending on the borrower's circumstances and income. Once working, borrowers have the option to postpone or reduce payments if they are having financial difficulty.

There are different types of federal student loan, as follows:

- **Direct Subsidized loans:** These are for undergraduate students who need financial aid, and the government pays the interest while the student is still studying.
- **Direct Unsubsidized loans:** These are for undergrads, graduates, and professional students, regardless of financial need. The interest charges are higher on these loans.
- **Direct Plus loans:** These are also for undergrads, graduates,

and professional students. The maximum loan amount is the cost of the study program the student is enrolled in.

- **Direct Consolidation loans:** These are for anyone who has more than one federal student loan and wants to combine them into one loan.

Private Student Loans

Some students take out private student loans. These work like any other loan. Borrowers apply for the loan and if approved, a lump sum is paid directly to their school. It covers their tuition fees, room and board, and any other student expenses. Any leftover money can be used for personal expenses. The interest rate can be fixed or variable. Sometimes, lenders will offer a lower interest rate while the person is in school and during a period after graduation. When the person starts repaying the loan, usually once they're working, the interest rate can go up.

Mastering Money

As with any loan, you need to read the fine print terms and conditions very carefully when taking out a student loan. Be sure you understand what repayment options are available and when you would need to start repaying your loan. Having student debt as an adult is not great, so find out how you can pay your student loan quicker. Also find out what would happen if you miss a loan payment. There are services in place to help in these situations.

Once you start working, you'll need to start paying off your student loan. This means you'll probably need to take another look at your budget to make sure you can make the repayments.

Get Financially Fit:

Pay Off Debt like a Pro

Expert Tips!

At some point in your life you may go into unmanageable debt. You may have spent too much on your credit card. Perhaps there was an emergency that you needed a personal loan for. Added to a student loan or an auto loan, and you may end up owing a lot of money. Here's what the experts say about paying off your debt.

Figure Out What Works for You

There is no one-size-fits-all approach to getting out of debt. You need to figure out what works best for you and your situation. The first thing you need to do is make a list of all your debt, the repayments, and the interest you're charged on that debt. Then you need to understand the different ways to pay off debt to figure out what will be best for you.

Being in debt can feel overwhelming until you figure out how to get on top of it.

Use the Snowball Method

In the snowball method of repaying debt, you pay off the smallest debt first, the one that's easiest to pay off. When you've done that, the money you were using for that repayment gets added to the next-smallest loan's repayment. You then pay off that loan and keep going until you're eventually debt free. As you take money from the smallest debt to the largest, the money available snowballs and grows. The snowball method works for many people because it's quick. You'll also feel great when you pay off a loan and that gives you the confidence to pay off the next debt you have.

Try Avalanche Repayments

The avalanche method starts with the biggest debt first, the one with the highest interest charges. When that's paid off, the spare money you have is used to pay off the second-highest debt. You keep going until you're debt free. With the avalanche method, you'll save money in the long term because you'll pay less interest. But it's not a quick fix so you'll need patience and careful budgeting.

Wrap It up with Consolidation

Consolidation means to combine many things to get one more effective, single item. This is exactly what happens when you consolidate your debt. You take all your debt and lump it together in one larger loan. Often the new loan's interest will be lower than all the interest you were paying before, so you'll save money. For many people, it's a relief to only have to manage just one loan at any one time.

It's All in the Budget

As you're working through your debt, try to understand how you got there in the first place. What steps can you take to make sure that it doesn't happen again? Go back to the previous chapter and reread the notes on budgeting. Set up a revised budget and do your best to keep to it.

Many people dream of owning a large house but big houses come with high repayments. It may be better to own a smaller home that you can comfortably afford.

Buying a Home

A home loan, or mortgage, is the biggest cause of debt. It makes sense to borrow money to buy a home though. People want to buy their own homes and few people have enough to pay cash for their property in one go up front.

So, How Do Mortgages Work?

Mortgages are secured installment loans. The home is the collateral. So the borrower must pay their monthly installments or the lender can foreclose on the property. This means they take back the property. The repayments will include interest, either at a fixed rate or a variable rate, depending on the terms of the loan.

A Mortgage Application

Because the credit a person is asking for is so large, mortgage providers need to make sure the borrower can pay back the money. The borrower will need to provide documents to help their application. These will include bank statements, letters of employment to show that they have a stable job, and pay stubs. Sometimes, home hunters will apply for a mortgage before they've found their dream place. The lender can pre-approve a mortgage. That means when the buyers come to purchase their house, they are at an advantage because the seller knows they have the money lined up.

Mastering Money

If debt helps you to increase your income or build your net worth—how much wealth you have—it's called good debt. Here are three examples of good debt:

- **Student loans:** These loans are often seen as good debt because the more educated you are, the greater your earning potential. With a further education, you'll be less likely to be unemployed too.
- **Mortgages:** Most homes increase in value as time goes on, so you could sell your home for a profit or rent it to create an income.
- **Business loans**: Starting a new business is risky but if the risk pays off, your business could make you a lot of money.

Types of Mortgage

Most people pay a down payment to reduce the loan amount. The rest of the house price is paid for through a mortgage. A fixed-rate mortgage is also called a traditional mortgage and it's the most common. In this type of mortgage, the interest stays the same. In an adjustable rate mortgage, the interest is fixed for a term then it changes. At first the interest rate is often below market rates, so makes the mortgage more appealing. However, at some point it rises above market rates. The third type of mortgage is an interest-only loan. The borrower pays off only the interest and then pays a large amount at the end of the term.

Getting a new business off the ground is a big financial risk. If the business does well, the risk will be worth it.

Future Credit and Debt Made Easy

You've reached the end of the book. By now you should understand a lot more about credit and debt, and here is one last recap.

Installment Credit Is Used for Larger Purchases

Big items (such as education, cars, and houses) that cost thousands of dollars need to be paid off in installments. Borrowers pay a set amount each month until the debt is paid. The interest charged on installment credit can vary a lot. It can also make a huge difference to your budget.

A One-Way Ticket to Debt

Banks offer personal loans for things like weddings, unexpected emergencies, and to pay medical bills. These are unsecured loans. Although they may seem like a good idea at the time, taking out a personal loan to pay for life's luxuries is not a credit-savvy thing to do. They put you in unnecessary debt.

Taking Out Loans for Vehicles

Most people take out an auto loan to pay for cars. Auto loans use the car as collateral. If a payment is missed, the vehicle can be repossessed by the lender.

Education Is Worth the Debt

A student loan is considered good debt. Education will increase your future employment options and earning potential. There are federal and private student loans that offer different repayment options, depending on your needs.

Pay Back Your Debt

If you do go into debt, you need to try to get yourself out of it as soon as possible. The three ways to do this are using the snowball method, avalanche method, or by consolidating your debts. Everyone's needs are different so deciding which method to use takes a lot of thought and careful budgeting.

Mortgages Lead to Owning Homes

Owning a home is a very adult thing to do but most adults need a mortgage to do this. There are different types of mortgage. Whichever one you choose, buying property is a long-term investment, and a long-term debt.

Now you know how to manage loans and credit, use those skills to make credit a tool that can help you build your financial future.

Glossary

anxious being worried, nervous, or uneasy about something
authorized having official permission or approval
auto-pay a payment method that automatically transfers money on a scheduled basis
balance the amount of money following a transaction
benefits advantages and profits gained from something
contracts legally-binding written or spoken agreements
cosign to sign a financial agreement with another person, accepting shared responsibility
credit bureaus companies that collect and maintain credit history information
deposit a sum of money placed in a bank account or used as security or collateral for a transaction
depression a mental health condition marked by prolonged sadness and loss of interest in things
discounts price reductions offered on goods or services
discriminate to treat someone differently because of where they come from, their sex, age, or disability
eligible meeting requirements to qualify for something
expenses money needed to do or buy something
insurance an arrangement by which a company promises to provide compensation for a specific loss, damage, illness, or death, in return for a payment called a premium
interest money paid regularly at a particular rate for money lent or earned
investing putting money into a financial scheme, shares, property, or business to make a profit
pay stubs documents sent to employees that show how much they have earned and what money has been deducted or taken off their salary
percentage a number expressed as a fraction of 100
postpone to delay or reschedule an event or payment
profit the difference between the money earned and spent in buying, operating, or producing something
purchase the act of buying something
realtors professionals who assist in buying, selling, or renting properties
repayment plan a structured plan that shows when money will be repaid to a lender
repossess to retake possession of something when the payments are missed
retail the industry involved in the sale of goods or services
return the gain or loss on an investment over a specific period
risk possibility of a loss
salary a fixed regular payment for work, often monthly
scam a dishonest scheme
secured credit cards credit cards requiring a deposit as collateral
security protection against risks or threats
subscriptions paid memberships or recurring purchases for services or products
tax monies paid to the government so that it can provide services
tuition fees payments required for education at schools or universities

Find Out More

Books

Explore other *Money Matters* books to find out more about how to make your money work for you:

Eason, Sarah. *Budgeting* (Money Matters). Cheriton Children's Books, 2026.

Eason, Sarah. *Saving* (Money Matters). Cheriton Children's Books, 2026.

Sanderson, Jennifer. *Jobs and Taxes* (Money Matters). Cheriton Children's Books, 2026.

Websites

The Credit Counselling Society offers help for anyone in debt or needing help understanding credit. You can find them at:
https://nomoredebts.org

Access financial advice from Credit Karma at:
www.creditkarma.com/advice

Be money smart by visiting the Practical Money Skills site at:
www.practicalmoneyskills.com/en

Publisher's note to educators and parents:
All the websites featured above have been carefully reviewed to ensure that they are suitable for students. However, many websites change often, and we cannot guarantee that a site's future contents will continue to meet our high standards of educational value. Please be advised that students should be closely monitored whenever they access the Internet.

Index

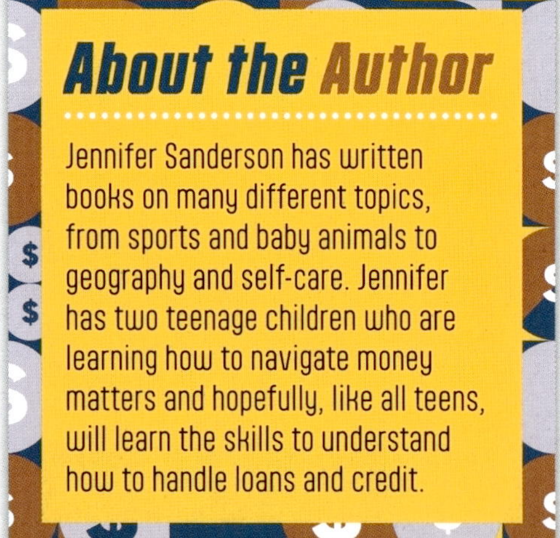

About the Author

Jennifer Sanderson has written books on many different topics, from sports and baby animals to geography and self-care. Jennifer has two teenage children who are learning how to navigate money matters and hopefully, like all teens, will learn the skills to understand how to handle loans and credit.